MAGGIE MARMELSTEIN
for
PRESIDENT

by

Marjorie Weinman Sharmat

Pictures by Ben Shecter

Orlando   Boston   Dallas   Chicago   San Diego

Visit *The Learning Site!*
www.harcourtschool.com

The recipe for Victory Cake on pages 121–22
was given to Mrs. Marmelstein
by the author's father, Mr. Nathan Weinman.

This edition is published by special arrangement with
HarperCollins*Children'sBooks,* a division of HarperCollins Publishers, Inc.

Grateful acknowledgment is made to HarperCollins*Children'sBooks,*
a division of HarperCollins Publishers, Inc. for permission to reprint
Maggie Marmelstein for President by Marjorie Weinman Sharmat,
illustrated by Ben Shecter, cover illustration by Alan Tiegreen.
Text copyright © 1975 by Marjorie Weinman Sharmat;
illustrations copyright © 1975 by Ben Shecter;
cover illustration © 1991 by Alan Tiegreen.

Printed in the United States of America

ISBN   0-15-314427-0

2   3   4   5 6   7   8   9   10   060   03   02   01

for Cary Grant
even though
he didn't call again
472–3418

Contents

1

Thad Smith Needs Help

Maggie Marmelstein thought that Thad Smith could be a good president for the sixth grade. "Not great, just good," she thought. "Thad Smith is not ready for greatness. I can tell by the way his T-shirt hangs down and a piece of his hair sometimes sticks up. I can tell by the peanut-butter-and-ketchup sandwiches he brings to school."

Maggie was sitting in her social studies classroom while Mr. Krickleman, the teacher, explained the rules for the campaign for president of the sixth grade.

"Anyone who wishes to run for president must have a petition signed by at least fifteen members of the sixth grade," he said. "Each candidate should be prepared to make speeches, discuss issues and do all those things any candidate for office does. But no candidate is allowed to give gifts. This includes buttons, pens, shopping bags, et cetera."

Maggie raised her hand. "A good candidate wouldn't need all that junk anyway. A good candidate just needs a good manager."

"Thank you for that interesting thought, Maggie," said Mr. Krickleman.

Maggie looked at Thad. She was sure he was going to run for president. She was sure because he was busy yawning too hard while his feet were doing a private little dance. He was going to try for president all right. He was also scared of the idea. Maggie was sure of that, too.

"Thad Smith is not a terrific speaker," thought Maggie. "Thad Smith does not come on strong. Thad Smith is not who you think of when you think of a head of state, head of class or head of anything. He needs help. I could help him. I could be his manager."

Noah Moore raised his hand. "May a student sign as many petitions as he or she wishes?" he asked. "If not, there will be a massive stampede after class to obtain signatures as quickly as possible. To hog them, you might say."

Ronald the Rock Thrower yelled, "Everybody be a hog. Stampede! Stampede!"

Mr. Krickleman ignored Ronald. "Noah has made an excellent point, as usual," he said. "A student may sign as many petitions as he or she wishes. But please do think before signing."

The bell rang, and class was over. Outside the classroom everyone gathered in little groups. A couple of kids announced they were running for president.

Maggie's best friend Ellen came up to her. "I wouldn't want to be president of anything," she said. "Would you?"

"There's a better job than president," said Maggie.

"What's that?"

"I can't tell you right now."

"Okay, but if you want to tell me later, I'll be glad to hear it later," said Ellen. "Say, it looks like Thad Smith is running. Look at him over there with all those kids around him. He's got his arms raised like a candidate, unless he's shooing away flies. But flies are out of season now, so he must be running. What do you think about that?"

"Should I think about it?" asked Maggie.

"Well, you and Thad are sort of friends, but sometimes you're sort of enemies, so I was wondering if you feel friendly about his running for president."

"I feel friendly about that," said Maggie. "It's really a very good idea that he wants to be a candidate."

"I think so, too," said Ellen, "so I'm glad you think so."

Maggie and Ellen walked up to Thad's group. Thad was in the middle of it. His best friend Henry was standing next to him, calling, "Over here, everybody, for a free speech by Thad Smith. No admission charge. Hurry, hurry, while the spaces last."

Thad Smith said, "I want to thank all of you for filling up so many spaces. Thank you. I have never run for anything before. But now I want to be president because . . ."

Thad stopped. He didn't seem to know what to say next.

Maggie said, "Because you can do more for the sixth grade."

Maggie was pleased that her first chance to manage Thad had come so soon. Thad looked at her in an interested way.

"What can you do, Thad?" asked someone in the group.

Thad didn't say anything.

"What can you do?" somebody asked again.

"Well," said Thad, "look in the Yellow Pages of the phone book. I can do most everything listed in the Yellow Pages."

Maggie groaned. Thad needed lots of managing.

2

Decision in the Laundry Room

Maggie was glad that she and Thad Smith lived on the same floor of the same apartment house. She thought it would make it easier to find the right chance to tell him in private that she would be his manager for the campaign. Her chance came that night while she was in the laundry room with two loads of dirty laundry.

She was starting to sort it when Thad walked in with an overflowing basket. "Your towels are escaping," she said, "and your pillowcases are following them. I'd send for the police if I were you."

Then Maggie stroked one of Thad's towels as if it were a friendly dog. "I didn't know you did laundry, Thad," she said.

"I don't," said Thad. "Sometimes, like a couple of times a year, I help my parents with the laundry. But I don't fool around with sorting or stains or presoak. I don't even know what you're making with those piles. That's how much I don't do laundry. I'm just a dumper and a puller outer. I use the same muscles I use for tennis."

Thad picked up a piece of underwear and swung his arm back and then swung the underwear toward the opening of the washing machine. He missed.

Thad picked up the piece of underwear and swung again. He missed.

"Warm-up," he said.

But Maggie didn't seem interested in what he was doing. She didn't laugh. She didn't say anything, she just stared into space. Then she turned toward Thad. "I have decided to do you a favor," she said.

"I can do my own laundry," said Thad.

"No, a real favor," said Maggie. "A big one."

"What kind of big one?"

"I am going to help you be class president," said Maggie.

"How?"

"By being your manager. I know how to manage."

"You want *me* to win?" Thad asked.

"I want *me* to manage," said Maggie.

Thad stared at his father's underwear, hoping to find the right thing to say somewhere in the wrinkles. He did not want Maggie to be his manager. Maggie was too strong. She would end up giving orders and he would end up taking them.

"Why don't you manage somebody else?" he said. "A good manager can manage anybody."

"Because I know you, Thad Smith. I know what you can do and what you can't do. I know where you're strong and where you're jellyfish. I can hide your jellyfish."

"I'm not jellyfish anywhere," said Thad. "And I already have a fantastic manager who knows that."

"Who? Henry? Henry couldn't manage an ice-cream cone from dripping."

"Henry can manage an ice-cream cone, and Henry can manage me," said Thad. He spread his arms wide. "Look, there's plenty you can manage instead of me. Socks! Shirts! Pajamas! Towels! Underwear! They need decisions—detergent, timing, arranging. Boy, do they need managing."

"You're turning my favor down?" asked Maggie. "You're turning down your chance to be president?"

"Yes to the first part, no to the second," said Thad.

Maggie felt like running from the room. If only she could start the conversation all over again. If only she could go back to its beginning. She wanted Thad to enter the laundry room all over

7

again. Maybe he would trip over his laundry basket this time. The big thing would be that this time she would say to him, "Your towels are escaping and I would never be your manager even if you begged me." She wanted to say anything that would hurt Thad Smith.

But it was too late. Thad said, "Did you *manage* to be here in the laundry room the same time as me when I'm only here two times a year?"

"I was here first," said Maggie. "And you came in. And you couldn't even manage *your* laundry. You're a person who needs help."

"Not your help. Ever," said Thad.

"Okay," Maggie said. "You just lost the election."

"Here?" said Thad. "Here in the laundry room?"

"Right here," said Maggie. "Because right here and now, Thad Smith, somebody else has decided to run for president. Somebody who's full of great ideas. Somebody who's going to win. How does this sound: *Maggie Marmelstein for president.*"

Thad Smith took a step backward, almost losing his balance.

Maggie wished he could stay that way forever. Like a silly statue. Maybe some day a whole monument could be erected in the laundry room to show the very place where she had made her

decision to run for president of the sixth grade and had told Thad Smith about it. "Nothing too conspicuous," she thought. "Just me in solid bronze standing tall over my tub of permanent press, also in solid bronze, and Thad Smith, fainting, in some sort of chipping plastic."

Maggie started the washing machine and left the room.

3

Fifteen Friendly Faces

Maggie Marmelstein sat in her bedroom. She looked at the pictures of movie actors that were all over the walls. "Who wants to hear the latest news?" she asked. She got up and walked over to Steve McQueen, John Wayne and Paul Newman. She stopped in front of Cary Grant. She spoke. "Thad Smith, whom you do not know, underrates me. *Me*, Maggie Marmelstein. He probably thinks I'm too dumb to be his manager. But I'm not. *Maggie Marmelstein* and *dumb* don't go together. Inside Maggie Marmelstein there is a great brain, and great ideas come from it. I also have good red blood, strong bones, muscle, all kinds of stuff that can't easily be seen on the surface. Thad Smith has no idea that I have all these things. He doesn't pay any attention to me except in the wrong way. But I have got, inside and out, everything it takes to run for president of the sixth grade. And Mr. Grant—Cary—I will show Thad Smith!"

Maggie went to school early the next day. In her pocket she had a blank petition for running for president. She needed fifteen signatures on it.

As she walked along, she asked herself over and over, "How could Thad turn me down?" Maggie couldn't ask anyone else. She didn't want anyone else to know. She wondered if Thad would tell Henry.

"Maybe he'll brag and say, 'Guess who offered to do what for me.' Well, let him tell Henry. If Henry has a brain in his head, he'll tell Thad he turned down a good deal. However, Henry does not have a brain in his head, so that takes care of that."

When Maggie got to school she started to look for fifteen friendly faces. The first friendly face she saw belonged to Ellen.

"Oh, Ellen, you're number one to sign," she said.

"Another petition for president," said Ellen, without looking at the paper. "I've already signed six."

"Six?" said Maggie. "Why did you sign so many?"

"Because six kids asked me," said Ellen. "And it's easier to say yes than no. And it's all legal. A person can sign as many petitions as the person wants."

Ellen looked down at the paper. "Oh, Maggie, I didn't know that *you* were running for president. I would have said no to the other six people. I could have done it, really. I would have taken a deep breath and looked them straight in the eye and said NO!"

"Was Thad Smith one of the six you said yes to?" asked Maggie.

"Sure," said Ellen.

"Could you sort of cross off your name?" asked Maggie. "It would be good practice, Ellen. Crossing off your name and saying no are practically the same thing."

Ellen sighed. "I think it's too late for any crossing off. I sort of saw Thad hand in his petition. Anyway, I thought that you thought it was a good idea for Thad to run for president. Isn't that what you said yesterday?"

"Yesterday I was dumb. Today I'm smart," said Maggie. "And today I'm running for president."

Ellen signed the petition and handed it back to Maggie. "See, I wrote my name in very very large letters," she said. "I hope you win, Maggie, and I'll help you all I can."

"Think of some other people who can't say no," said Maggie.

Then Ellen and Maggie both said together, "Noah!"

"I'll go find him," said Ellen. "Wait right here."

"I'm not going anywhere," said Maggie. But she wished she were. Suddenly she felt silly standing against a wall hoping for the right kids to come along.

"I wish I were a famous actress on a stage," she thought, "and everybody else was down below. And they'd all come up to me and *ask* to sign my petition."

Maggie saw Cynthia Stauffeur. "Have you heard the news?" Maggie said. "I'm running for president and this is my petition and I'd like you to sign it."

"I've already signed one," said Cynthia.

"One?" said Maggie. "Is that all? Ellen signed seven, including mine. It's easier to say yes than no."

"No," said Cynthia.

"No?"

"No," said Cynthia. "Because it's easier to say no once you've said yes. But good luck, Maggie."

Cynthia walked away.

Ellen came running up with Noah. "Look who I've got," she said. "And he's only signed three others, and he won't sign any more after yours."

Noah took a green pen out of his pocket. "It writes green, too," he said. "I always sign in green.

Someday if this becomes a historical document, my name will be noticed like John Hancock's was."

Noah looked at Maggie's petition. "You only have Ellen's signature here," he said. "And mine."

"I'm just getting started," said Maggie. "I'm waiting for the right people to come along."

"Historically the wrong people often turn out to be the right people," said Noah. "Take, for example, Ronald the Rock Thrower, over there. He is not anyone's idea of the right person."

Noah went up to Ronald. "Ronald, Maggie Marmelstein is running for class president, and she wants you to sign her petition!"

Ronald didn't say anything. He took out a pencil and wrote something on Maggie's petition. He kept writing.

Maggie ran over and grabbed the paper from him. "What are you doing, Ronald?"

"Signing my name five times," said Ronald. "One time is good, two times is great, three times is terrific, four times is unbelievably fantastic, and five times is—"

"Illegal," said Noah. "But thanks for the first time."

"Sure," said Ronald, and walked away. Noah erased the extra signatures.

"Noah, you're the one who is unbelievably fantastic," said Maggie. "Nobody else would ask Ronald."

"That's why I did," said Noah. "Now let's keep going."

Noah walked up to Jody Klinger, who was so fat that if she signed her name five times it would seem as if she were signing for just a fraction of herself.

Noah said something to her, she said something to Noah, Noah said something back to her and she signed.

"Jody Klinger," thought Maggie. "The only time I ever spoke to her was when I offered her a low-cal soda and she gave me a dirty look."

Noah disappeared into a crowd of kids. Soon he was back waving the petition. "Twelve down and three to go," he said.

"Noah, I know you're the smartest kid in the sixth grade, but how could you get so many signatures so soon?"

"I simply told everybody it was their last chance to sign Maggie Marmelstein's petition," said Noah.

"But, Noah, it's their first chance."

"That's also true," said Noah.

"Noah," said Maggie, "every candidate needs

a manager. Even me. Be my campaign manager. Please."

"I can't," said Noah. "Someone else asked me just this morning and I turned him down."

"Who asked you?"

"Thad Smith," said Noah.

"Thad Smith? Thad Smith asked you?" Maggie raised her voice. "Henry is his manager."

"No, he isn't," said Noah. "Thad said that Henry is a great guy, but he couldn't manage an ice-cream cone from dripping. Those were his exact words."

"Not exactly his," said Maggie Marmelstein.

4

A Mole-a-gram

Maggie sat behind Noah in math class and stared at the mole on the back of his neck. Maggie considered the mole to be a trademark of high intelligence and significant thoughts. Sometimes she had an urge to press on it, hoping it would make a buzzing sound heard only by her and Noah, and then she and Noah could communicate via mole messages. Today she wanted to press it and say, "Now hear this, Noah. Thad Smith is a schnook. *I* told him Henry couldn't keep an ice-cream cone from dripping and *I* offered to be his manager and he turned me down, and then he asked *you*."

No, she couldn't say that. She didn't want Noah or anyone to know she had been turned down. How about a short mole note? "Buzzzzz. I have a mole-a-gram for you, sir:

DEAR NOAH, THAD SMITH A SCHNOOK. EVIDENCE OF SAME CANNOT BE REVEALED. TRUST ME. BE MY MANAGER. I LIKE YOUR MOLE. SIGNED, MAGGIE MARMELSTEIN. P.S. PLEASE ANSWER."

Maggie opened her math book and pretended to work hard for the rest of the period.

After class she followed Noah out of the room and caught up with him. "Noah," she said, "I know something that if you knew it, you would be my manager. So will you?"

"That sounds mysterious," said Noah. "If I were acquainted with all aspects of this secret, would I become your manager?"

"Huh?" said Maggie.

"I want to know if there is something unpleasant, sneaky, demoralizing, unjust or frightening going on that I am not aware of that would cause me to become your manager."

"Yep," said Maggie.

"Which one?"

"Sneaky and unjust," said Maggie. "That sums it up. I can't say any more."

"That's sufficient," said Noah. He held out his hand. "You can shake hands with your new manager if you wish."

"Shake," said Maggie. She had never shaken hands with anyone her own age. It made her feel like a candidate.

"I'll meet you in the library after school, and we'll discuss strategy," said Noah.

"The library? I don't like to whisper," said Maggie. "I can't think right when I whisper."

"I think best when I'm surrounded by thinkers," said Noah. "This library is full of thinkers who put their thoughts between covers."

"Okay, I'll be there," said Maggie. "Oh, Noah, are you going to tell Thad that you're my manager?"

"Of course," said Noah.

"How are you going to tell him? What will you say?"

"I haven't chosen my words yet," said Noah.

"I'll tell him for you," said Maggie. "I'll do that for you, Noah."

"No, that's my responsibility," said Noah.

"But you don't really want to tell him, and I do," said Maggie.

Noah stared at Maggie. "Maggie," he said, "is there some reason in addition to sneaky and unjust why you want me to be your manager?"

"Oh, no," said Maggie. "That's it."

"Splendid," said Noah. "I'll tell him myself."

After school Maggie went to the library. Noah was sitting at the far end of the room. He spent more time in the library than any other kid in school. He had a certain chair that he liked to sit in, and most of the other library kids left it vacant for him. Mrs. Bromley, the librarian, loved him. He was her best customer, her quietest customer, and if he found a book in the wrong alphabetical

order, he put it in its correct place with a great flourish.

"You're a treasure, Noah," Mrs. Bromley whispered over and over.

Some of the kids used the library as a hangout, and Mrs. Bromley, declaring that the library should be "both a fun and learning place," encouraged them to come. But she watched those kids closely.

"Hello, Mrs. Bromley," said Maggie.

"Hello," said Mrs. Bromley. She watched Maggie closely.

Maggie started to walk toward Noah, who was bent over some books, when she heard someone shout, "Maggie Marmelstein!"

"Shh," said Maggie, as she turned around to see who had shouted to her. It was Thad.

"Noah just told me he's your manager," said Thad. "Did you know I was kidding with him this morning and asked him to be my manager? But Henry's my manager. I wouldn't run for president if I didn't have Henry."

"Run like a dripping ice-cream cone!" said Maggie.

Mrs. Bromley was still watching.

Maggie hurried toward Noah.

"Ah, you're here," whispered Noah. "I've already formed our beginning strategy. Please write down the name of every friend who might vote for you. And every *potential* friend. Potential is very important. Untapped people. Possibilities. They can make the difference." Noah gave Maggie a long blank piece of paper. "Please start writing."

Maggie wrote *Ellen.* Then she put her pencil down.

"That's it?" whispered Noah. "Attila the Hun had more friends than that. His friendships are not generally publicized, but I found fascinating material about them."

"I have a lot of friends," said Maggie, "but most of them are also friends with the other seven kids running for president."

"Four," said Noah. "Three candidates have already dropped out. They were jokers. They used the backs of labels from giant cans of tomato juice for their petitions."

"Did you sign the tomato-juice petitions, Noah?"

"Well, yes," whispered Noah, looking away from Maggie. "I thought they represented a new approach to ecology. At any rate, I suggest you make up a list of people and invite them to a meeting at your house. Tomorrow after school."

"Tomorrow?" Maggie said. "So soon?"

"Definitely. Before the other candidates get to them."

"You're a genius, Noah," said Maggie.

"No. True genius usually isn't apparent," said Noah. "It hides in the depths of great intelligence and only comes out in specialized circumstances. But thank you for thinking of me in that way."

"Oh, Noah, I like you!" said Maggie.

Mrs. Bromley looked up, but didn't say "Shh." Since she liked Noah, too, she was glad to see him get public acclaim.

Thad Smith looked up. Then down.

"He can't stand it that I've got the best brain in the sixth grade for my manager," thought Maggie.

"I'll go home and make a big list," Maggie whispered to Noah. "Then should I call up the names?"

"No. You must delegate tasks like that."

"I'll ask Ellen to call them."

"Ellen doesn't like to ask anybody to do anything," whispered Noah.

"I know it," said Maggie. "But she won't be asking for herself. This is just the kind of asking practice she needs."

"Clever!" said Noah, raising his voice. "You know, Maggie, you might have a touch of genius yourself."

Maggie looked at Thad, hoping he had overheard what Noah said. Thad didn't look up.

"It's too soon to tell if I'm a genius," Maggie announced.

Thad kept his head bent. He kept it bent as he stood up and walked out of the library.

5

Tamara Talks Talks Talks to Thad

Thad Smith went to the playground to shoot baskets. He missed every time but one.

Tamara Axelrod came along, stopped, watched and clapped.

"How come you're clapping when I'm missing?" asked Thad.

"I'm clapping because you're *trying*," said Tamara. "It's important to try, try, try."

"I think it's important to get the basketball in the basket," said Thad. "Missing is dumb."

"I don't think anything you do is dumb," said Tamara.

"Well, don't watch me while I'm missing," said Thad. "If I have a good streak, I'll let you know."

"I like watching you," said Tamara. "I think you're super, super, super."

Thad looked at Tamara. "Only my mother thinks I'm super," he said. "And hardly ever three times in a row."

"Let's talk about the campaign," said Tamara.

"What about it?"

"Well, I think you'd make a splendiferous president."

"I never heard of that word," said Thad. "Is it better or worse than great? Like give me an example. Like could a jellyfish be splendiferous?"

"Never," said Tamara.

Thad tossed the ball toward the basket. He missed. "Maggie Marmelstein is running for president," he said. "That doesn't bother me at all. But if something did bother me, it would be that."

"Maggie Marmelstein will lose," said Tamara.

"How do you know that?" asked Thad. "She's smart and she could be splendiferous. You can't tell for sure, can you?"

"*You'll* win," said Tamara. She put her hand on Thad's arm. "Because I'll help with your campaign."

"How?" asked Thad.

"Oh, in simply tons and tons and tons of ways," said Tamara.

"Okay," said Thad. "You can help if you want to."

"Wonderful!" said Tamara. She kept her hand on Thad's arm.

She and Thad were too busy talking to notice that someone had been watching them from the far side of the playground. It was Maggie Marmel-stein, on her way home from school. Maggie walked on.

"Well, Thad Smith's no genius," she thought. "Anybody who likes Tamara Axelrod has got to be dopey."

Maggie left the playground. She didn't want to think about Thad and Tamara. But the more she didn't want to think about them, the more she did.

6

Snowflakes and Frozen Pizza

"I'll make you a victory cake for tomorrow's meeting," said Mrs. Marmelstein.

"But I haven't won yet," said Maggie. "And there are five other kids running."

"You'll win," said Mrs. Marmelstein. "Weren't you the princess in the class play last year? That's the top job in the kingdom except for the older folks. So this year you'll get the top job again, Madam President."

"Thad Smith is running, too."

"Oh, my frog friend," said Mrs. Marmelstein. "He's running? Last year he wanted to be frog, this year he wants to be president?"

"He likes variety," said Maggie. "This year he even likes arm grabbers."

Maggie went to her room to make a list of friends to invite to her meeting. She looked at the pictures on her wall. "Wish me luck, Cary Grant,

John Wayne, Rock Hudson, Paul Newman and Steve McQueen," she said to them.

She put the piece of paper with Ellen's name on it on her desk. She sat down and stared at the paper. "I'll just let names float into my head, like snowflakes coming down, until I have a big pile to write under *Ellen*. Tamara Axelrod. Tamara Axelrod? I shouldn't. I shouldn't. What was she up to with Thad anyway? If I invite her, maybe I'll find out. No! I will *not* invite her. The first snowflake will be Derek Flanders. He always wants to borrow my homework because I'm smarter than he is. I always turn him down, drat it. Also, his dog kissed me once and I told him that his dog had halitosis, which was true, but Derek said, 'It's better than having a big mouth like yours, Maggie Marmelstein.' Forget Derek Flanders.

"Maybe I should invite Tamara Axelrod. Tamara slobbers all over me and tells me I'm 'marvelous' and my hair looks 'terrific' and it's so 'wonderful' to have a friend like me. She says the same thing to everybody. Tamara gives away millions of dollars' worth of words for a nickel's worth of results. But every campaign needs one gush person. And besides, she might gush out something important.

"No. 2: Dipsey Ford. Dipsey is one of those

hang-down kids who look as if they have a sadness in their lives that they are itching to tell you about if only you'd ask. I have never asked because I'm afraid of the answer. Invite her but don't ask questions.

"No. 3: Jody Klinger, low-cal snowflake. She *did* sign my petition. She's so fat that nobody ever gets past the fat to think of anything else about Jody. Fat is the beginning and end of Jody. But maybe there is a middle no one knows about. Invite her.

"No. 4: Ralph Nadesky. He was King Ralph in the play last year. Sometimes I call him Pops and he likes it. He must be nuts to like that, but invite him anyway."

Maggie wrote faster and faster. She remembered that Noah had told her there were forty-nine students in the sixth grade. If she had a small list, Noah might lose faith in her. But if her list were too big, she might get turned down too many times, and she would lose faith in herself. At last she had a list of twenty-one names. "Better than Attila the Hun for sure." She called Ellen.

"Ellen? Remember this morning when you said you would have taken a deep breath and looked kids straight in the eye and said NO! You said you would have done that for me."

"I remember," said Ellen.

"Now you've got a chance to do something for me that's much easier. Invite some kids to my house for tomorrow after school to talk about helping with my campaign."

"You mean I call them up and ask?"

"Yes. Isn't that easy? Tell them we'll have homemade cake and soda, too."

"Oh, a party. They'll like that."

"It's not a party. It's a campaign meeting with party food. Mention potato chips, too. And pretzels. Okay?"

"Well, I guess I could."

"Sound excited about it. Like it was a fantastic event."

"Okay. I'll even say 'fantastic event.' I just wrote that down. I'll write down what to say, and then I'll say it. But I'll make it sound not written down."

"Good. Now here's the list."

Maggie spoke slowly. When she got to name number twenty-one, she said quickly, "And Ronald Rathbone."

"Ronald the Rock Thrower? You want me to call *him*?" said Ellen. "I'd rather say no to a hundred people than call him."

"I need everybody I can get," said Maggie. "He signed my petition. Remember, he can't throw rocks through the telephone. Besides, I think he's stopped throwing rocks."

"Okay," said Ellen sadly.

"Thanks," said Maggie. "You're a real friend, Ellen."

"Yes, I believe that now," said Ellen. She sounded as if the phone had just captured her after a long chase and were tying her up in its cord.

"Good-bye," said Maggie. "See you tomorrow."

"Wait, don't hang up, Maggie. Let me try it out once on you. Hello, this is Ellen, and I'm inviting you to a fantastic event with homemade cake and potato chips and soda and pretzels to help Maggie Marmelstein be president. It's at her place tomorrow after school."

"Wonderful, wonderful!" said Maggie. Suddenly she sounded like Tamara Axelrod, and she hated herself.

She said good-bye to Ellen and went to the kitchen.

"I'm inviting twenty-one kids," she said to her mother.

"Then I'll make four times my recipe," said Mrs. Marmelstein. "I'm thinking of it as a victory cake, but I won't tell anybody out loud. I've got the ingredients in my head. I'll name them and you do the arithmetic times four and then meas-

ure them and hand them to me. I'll put them all together. Ready, set, go, Madam President. One half can of pumpkin times four."

"That was easy," said Maggie. She handed two cans of pumpkin to her mother.

"Thank you. Why do you want to be president, Maggie? Six dates times four. One half cup brown sugar times four. One very big grab of pecans times four."

"What do you mean, why?" Maggie asked.

"One small grab of raisins times four. Well, I know why you wanted to be princess last year. You always wanted to be an actress, a professional star, all shiny and bright up there on the stage. But president is brand-new to me. Two eggs times four."

"It's hard to explain. It's complicated," said Maggie, grabbing raisins and counting eggs.

"One small grab of sunflower seeds times four. Can you uncomplicate me, Maggie? Tell me— when you're president, what will you be doing? One half cup whole wheat flour times four. Baking soda and baking powder. I'll do the spoon mathematics for them."

"Doing? Why I'll be president of the sixth grade. That's what I'll be doing. I'll preside."

"But what will you *do* besides presiding? Can you offer any Maggie specialties? A few drops of orange juice times four. A few drops of sweet red wine times four. A salt shaker. I'll do the shaking. A banana times four. And for the bottom and sides of the pan, a swish of butter times four and a sprinkle of wheat germ times four."

"I haven't thought about my specialties yet," said Maggie. "You're out of bananas."

"They go fast. One minute I have a banana plantation. The next minute I'm bananaless," said Mrs. Marmelstein. "Maybe I can substitute."

"I'll get some more at the store," said Maggie. "I'm out of potato chips, so I have to go anyway."

Mrs. Marmelstein gave Maggie some money. "Ask Mr. Rossi how his sinuses are doing," said Mrs. Marmelstein. "Yesterday they weren't doing so well."

Maggie walked quickly to Rossi's Market. She was excited. "All those kids coming to *my* place," she thought, "to help *me* get to be president. But what if they all say no? No, they won't turn down Ellen. Turning down Ellen is like turning down a major charity. Ellen needs to succeed and everyone knows it. Everyone contributes a little something. Except Ronald. I should have called him myself."

Maggie went into the market. Mr. Rossi looked up.

"My mother wants to know how your sinuses

are today, Mr. Rossi." Maggie liked to get her mother's messages and questions over with quickly.

"Much better, tell your mother," said Mr. Rossi. "How's her feet?"

Maggie had been afraid she would get an exchange question.

"Her feet are neat," said Maggie. "They don't hurt this week."

Mr. Rossi smiled. "That's almost a poem," he said. "Well, Maggie, what can I do for you today?"

"I'm having a fantastic event tomorrow," said Maggie. "Maybe twenty-three kids. I need five giant bags of potato chips and one banana times four."

"That's a big armful for you to carry," said Mr. Rossi. He looked past Maggie. Someone had just come into the store and was standing behind her. "You're in luck, Maggie," said Mr. Rossi. "Here's somebody from your building who can help you carry home the goodies for your fantastic event tomorrow. Hello, Thad."

Maggie whirled around.

"Hello, Mr. Rossi. Hello, Maggie. A fan-tas-tic e-vent, how about that?" said Thad.

Thad and Maggie came to the same conclusion: Maggie talked too much.

Mr. Rossi went on. "Twenty-three kids. That's a big group."

"Sure is," said Thad, grateful for the extra information.

"What can I do for you, Thad?" asked Mr. Rossi.

"That you haven't already done," thought Maggie.

"I came for frozen pizza," said Thad. He looked in the freezer case. "I'll buy all you've got."

"I didn't know you were that crazy about pizza," said Mr. Rossi.

"Today I am," said Thad.

"Looks like you'll have a bigger armful than Maggie," said Mr. Rossi. "Maybe Maggie can help you carry."

"I do my own carrying," said Thad.

"So do I," said Maggie.

Maggie left the store before Thad. She walked slowly. She thought about all the frozen pizzas Thad had bought. They made her feel cold.

7

A Special Job for Thad

Maggie was waiting for Ellen at school the next morning.

"I didn't want to busy your line and call you last night," said Maggie. "How many kids are coming?"

Ellen didn't answer.

"What's the matter, Ellen?"

"Nothing."

"Are you holding your breath?"

"Yes."

"Why?"

"I forgot to brush my teeth. I'm so excited about your running for president that I forgot about my teeth. If I breathe out, I'll offend."

"Silly! Breathe! Breathe!"

"I always brush my teeth," said Ellen.

"I know it," said Maggie. "How many kids are coming?"

"I forgot to bring the list," said Ellen. "But so far, more kids are coming than not coming. And I have a few more left to ask. Now if I were you I would be happy that most of the kids are coming, but I wouldn't be *very* happy. See, some kids I called asked me if I was really positive there would be homemade cake and soda and potato chips and pretzels, and when I said yes they said they would come."

"Well, once we get the kids to the meeting, Noah will get them all excited about my campaign," said Maggie.

"I would get the kids all excited first and eat later if I were you," said Ellen. "Because if they eat first, they might leave before they can get all excited."

"Okay," said Maggie. "You're really into this, Ellen, and you're a big help. Could you ask the rest of the kids soon?"

"First, may I please breathe on you, and if it doesn't bother you, I won't have to hold my breath all day. It's hard to ask while you're holding."

"Sure, breathe," said Maggie.

Ellen put her face near Maggie's and breathed.

"You're in luck," said Maggie. "You had peanut butter for breakfast, didn't you? Peanut butter is one of the best smells to have."

Maggie looked for Noah. She told him that more kids were coming than not coming.

Ellen gave her report during the day. "Two more coming. Still peanut butter?"

"Still," said Maggie.

The last bell of the day rang and Maggie started to leave school. As she walked down the hall she saw Thad and Tamara leaning against a wall talking. "What are they doing buzz buzz buzzing again?" she wondered. "What are they doing together at all?" Maggie walked past them, using her princess walk, which was only for special occasions. Her head was high, her body erect, her powers absolute.

When Maggie got outside she began to run. She ran all the way home. She wanted to be there to greet all those kids who were going to help her win big over Thad Smith. "Just wait until I'm president of the sixth grade," she thought. "I'll give Thad Smith a very special job. He'll be the blackboard eraser person. PRESIDENT MAGGIE MAR- MELSTEIN will be printed all over every blackboard in school. And Thad Smith will erase it. And every time he erases it, it will instantly reappear. And fifty years from now he'll still be erasing, and it will still be reappearing."

When Maggie got to her apartment house, she

ran up the stairs to her floor. As she passed the door of Thad Smith's apartment she yelled, "Fifty years a blackboard eraser person! And it's your own fault, Thad Smith!"

8

Marmels-Team!

Noah arrived first. "How many are coming?" he asked as he walked into the foyer.

"Ellen wasn't sure," said Maggie. "She hadn't finished asking the last time I saw her today."

"Statistically, one has to expect a refusal rate of around thirty-five percent," said Noah, taking off his jacket.

"That high?" said Maggie. "Ellen told them we're having cake and soda and potato chips and pretzels."

"That may lower the percentage by as much as five to ten points," said Noah.

"My mother made the cake."

"Another possible five points if advertised," said Noah. "Where is your mother, by the way?"

"In the bedroom watching television. She's coming out when Ben Hur's race is over. She said she'd really rather watch you because you're ten times faster than Ben Hur's chariot. You sure did swing into action fast with this meeting, Noah. You are definitely a fast worker."

"No, I'm not," said Noah. "Working fast goes against all my principles. To do a really good job of running for president takes months and months. But we have only a short time, so I'm stuck with this quickie sort of business. But it's my first and last quickie undertaking, I'll tell you that."

The doorbell rang. Maggie opened the door. Ellen and Tamara were standing there. "We came together," said Ellen. "We met in the elevator, so we didn't come *all* the way together."

Tamara said, "I've come to help you win, win, win. I have three presidents in my family. My mother is president of the garden club, my father is president of L.V.O.—I don't know what that stands for, but it's very, very important. And my uncle is president of a dentists' club. Maggie, you look so *presidential* in that dress. Doesn't she, everybody?"

Everybody—Ellen and Noah—said yes.

"Let's everybody go into the living room," said Maggie.

"May I please have a glass of water?" said Noah.

"Sure," said Maggie. Ellen and Tamara walked into the living room. Maggie and Noah went to the kitchen. Maggie took a glass from the cupboard.

"She's a spy," said Noah.

"What? Who?" said Maggie, holding the empty glass in midair.

"Tamara," said Noah. "She's too friendly. Too loyal. I don't think she even likes you."

"True," said Maggie. "But if she's phony, she's phony to everybody."

"You believe she's consistently phony?" said Noah.

"Probably," said Maggie. "She talks to everybody the same way."

"No," said Noah. "I saw her with Thad today. She *looks* at Thad in a special way."

"How special?" Maggie put the empty glass down. "Does he look back that way? I'm asking because of the campaign."

"I'm not sure," said Noah. "But I'll keep watching."

"Do that," said Maggie. "And I'll watch, too."

"You forgot my water," said Noah.

"Oh, you really want it."

Maggie ran the hot tap and started to fill Noah's glass.

"I think I'd prefer cold," said Noah. "Or at least cool."

"Oh, sure," said Maggie. "Sorry."

The doorbell rang. Three boys and one girl arrived together. A few minutes later more boys and girls came. At last there were fifteen kids, including Maggie, Noah and Ellen, sitting around the living room, on the sofa, on chairs, on the floor.

"I forgot to tell you that I got nine turndowns," said Ellen. "One of them was Ronald. But he said he might help you. He said he had a big piece of cheese in his refrigerator which he's been eating for a week. Every day he takes a bite. If the cheese has grown some mold before the week is over, he will help you get to be president."

A few of the kids laughed.

"Never mind," said Noah. "It's better than rocks."

Maggie spoke up. "It's wise-guy and we all know it."

"Our leader! She speaks the truth," shouted Ralph Nadesky.

"Let's not talk about Ronald anymore," said Tamara. "Let's hear every little bit of your campaign plans. Every tiny, scrunchy, crunchy bit."

Maggie stood up. "As the future president of the sixth grade, I want to say that our plans don't scrunch, don't crunch."

Ralph laughed. "I never saw a scrunchy plan. But if I do I'll eat it."

Everybody laughed. Noah stood up. "Order. Order. Today we'll simply plan the basics. I'll pass out pencils and paper, and I'd like each of you to write down any campaign ideas you have and how you would like to help."

"I'd love to have a special assignment," said Tamara. "Like ordering campaign buttons or shopping bags or little souvenirs to give away."

"Tamara," said Noah, "the rules are that any candidate who gives gifts is disqualified."

"I didn't hear anything about *that*," said Tamara.

"You must have been in Alaska the last two days," said Ralph. "Wearing earmuffs."

Noah handed out pencils and paper. Everyone wrote something. Noah collected the papers and studied them.

"We have ideas for posters and slogans, and someone suggested a 'rousing song.' Good idea."

"Great," said Maggie. "A song about me."

"Hey," said Ralph. "How's this? A Song about Maggie: *Maggie, Maggie Marmelstein. Maggie, Maggie leads the team.*"

"Splendid. We could set that to music," said Noah.

"I don't like it," said Tamara. "How about *Maggie, Maggie Marmelstein. Maggie keeps her fingernails clean.*"

Noah and Maggie looked at each other, and then at Tamara. "I don't think that idea would help Maggie at all," said Noah. "It might hurt her."

"Really?" said Tamara. "Isn't the big thing that a campaign should be is *clean*?"

"Not down to its fingernails," said Noah.

Ellen said, *"Who loves Maggie? Everyone! And the stars, the moon, the sun!* No, wait. That's not good. *Who loves Maggie? The whole sixth grade. Maggie Marmelstein has*—uh—"

"Got it made!" shouted Maggie.

"Excellent but too optimistic," said Noah.

"How about this?" said Tamara. *"Who loves Maggie Marmelstein? Cary Grant and Steve Mc-Queen!"*

"No!" said Maggie. Tamara must have seen the pictures on her bedroom wall. She probably sneaked a peek when no one was looking.

Noah was also angry. "That idea," he said to Tamara, "stinks!"

"You've sure got plenty of lousy ideas, Tamara," said Mitchell Fritz. "You could go into the lousy-idea business with all those lousy ideas. You could get rich. Step right up, folks, and get your lousy ideas while they last. Red-hot lousy ideas. A dollar each."

"That's inflation," yelled Ralph.

48

"Order, order," said Noah.

"Well, I'm serious about this campaign," said Tamara, "which is more than I can say for some of you. I really, seriously want to know what your campaign promises will be, Maggie. Any new ideas for winning votes?"

Noah said quickly, "We've had enough ideas for today. But I'd like all of you to get your friends into Maggie's campaign. Get your musical friends to help with the song, your artistic friends to help with posters. And one last item. Our group should have a name. Ralph, your team idea could be used here also. What do you all think of MAR-MELS-TEAM? Join MARMELS-TEAM."

"Terrible," said Tamara.

"Perfect," said Maggie.

"Perfect," said Ralph.

"Perfect," said Ellen.

Noah took a vote. MARMELS-TEAM passed thirteen to two.

"I voted against it because it made me feel hungry," said Jody Klinger. "Certain words make me feel hungry. Like marshmallow, crunchy, wiggle, Transylvania, leaf and optician. And now MAR-MELS-TEAM."

Tamara laughed.

"It's not funny," said Maggie. Maggie knew that words had power. Every time she thought about the word Tamara, she wanted to vomit.

"The meeting is adjourned," said Noah.

"Food's in the kitchen," said Maggie. "Let's go."

Maggie, Noah and Ellen served the cake, soda, pretzels and potato chips. Maggie, watching everyone eat and drink, was happy to have this group, this *team* on her side. Maggie wanted to hug everyone in the room except Tamara. How terrific that they were getting their brains together just to help her. Sitting around *her* kitchen and on *her* team were brains, talent and energy.

And sneakiness.

"I have to leave," said Tamara, "and do my homework. But the meeting was thrilling. I didn't want to miss your meeting for anything in the world." Tamara walked toward the door. "Byebye, all you Marmels-teams."

Maggie watched Tamara go down the hall. She wondered if Tamara would stop at Thad's door. She didn't. "She'll hand in her report later," thought Maggie.

Suddenly the door to Thad's apartment opened and five kids walked out eating pizza crusts, followed by three more kids, and two more and three more. Maggie stood at her door counting. She lost count at sixteen.

They were all chanting, *"You'll be glad if you vote for Thad!"*

"Yikes!" thought Maggie Marmelstein. The cold feeling she had had yesterday when she saw Thad buying the frozen pizzas came back. "It isn't going to be easy to beat Thad, after all. The forces of evil can marshal even more support than the forces of good, especially when pizza is served."

But there was something much worse than Thad having his pizza meeting. There was something so scary that Maggie didn't want to think about it, but she had to. Thad and his group could keep a secret! A whole bunch of kids, loyal to Thad, could keep the secret of the pizza meeting. All those kids coming to his house and not breathing a word of it in advance around school. What Maggie needed was someone to spy on Thad's campaign. But no. Maggie didn't want to use a spy. She wanted to win the honest way, the hard way.

Maggie walked back into her apartment, smarter than she had been when she walked out of it seconds before.

9

We Do and We Don't

Maggie and Noah held an emergency breakfast meeting at Maggie's apartment at seven o'clock the next morning.

"Just the two of us," Noah had said. "And your mother. And her bread pudding."

Mrs. Marmelstein served the pudding hot and poured milk over it.

Noah started to eat. "This pudding has a fabulous taste and a fabulous texture," he said.

"Enjoy both of them," said Mrs. Marmelstein. "I'm enjoying attending your emergency breakfast meeting. I'm very interested."

Mrs. Marmelstein sat down. "I would like to ask the first, number one question of your emergency breakfast meeting," she said. "How many candidates are there?"

"Six," said Noah. "But Maggie and Thad are the strongest."

"Thank you. I have a second, number two question," said Mrs. Marmelstein. "What if somebody wants to vote for somebody who isn't a candidate?"

"Somebody can write somebody's name on the ballot," said Noah.

"The sixth grade is a real democracy," said Mrs. Marmelstein.

"Yes, it's a democracy we want Maggie to be president of," said Noah. He looked at Maggie. "The important thing is not to panic," he said. "Just because Thad Smith has a larger group of supporters."

"And a slogan. And a spy," said Maggie.

"I'm delighted about the spy," said Noah.

"What?" said Maggie.

"Well," said Noah, "she can transmit information for us. Information we *want* Thad to receive."

"Why don't we just tell Thad ourselves?" asked Maggie.

"Because we want him to think we don't want him to have the information," said Noah.

"What information?" asked Maggie.

"The information that we don't want a debate between you and Thad."

"We don't?"

"We do!" said Noah. "In fact, that is my major campaign plan, but I didn't want to reveal it yesterday. I *want* you and Thad to hold a debate. You're an excellent talker and you think quickly in front of an audience. Last year during the class play when Thad's frog suit slipped down, you were the one who thought of the right words to say to save the play."

"My Maggie was marvelous when the zipper wasn't," said Mrs. Marmelstein.

"Thad's afraid of an audience," said Maggie. "Before he went on the stage as the frog, his knees knocked, his voice cracked and his teeth went *click click*. I know he won't want to debate me." Maggie looked at Noah. "But *I* want to debate *him*. I feel at home on the stage. And knowing how nervous Thad is up there, well, that makes me like it even more. But Thad won't debate me, Noah. I'm positive."

"He will if he thinks it will hurt your campaign," said Noah. "Therefore, I'll tell Tamara the spy that we don't want a debate. Then she'll tell Thad, and he'll challenge us to a debate that we want that he thinks we don't want."

"When will you tell her?" asked Maggie.

"Today," said Noah. "But I won't actually tell her. I'll sort of let her dig the information out of me."

"Tamara's a great digger," said Maggie.

Noah stood up. "The emergency breakfast meeting is over," he said.

"I packed some bread pudding for you to take to school in case you have an emergency lunch meeting," said Mrs. Marmelstein. "Have a good day in your democracy. And Noah, be very careful getting dug."

10

Noah's Popsicle Plan

Noah sat on a bench in the park eating a Popsicle.

He was waiting for Tamara to come by. Tamara walked through the park on her way home from school when the weather was good. Tamara liked the park because it was "so greeny and fluffy."

"Well, hello, Noah." Tamara saw him before he saw her. "Why aren't you in the library?"

"I felt like eating a Popsicle under the trees," said Noah. "It's different from the library experience."

"I guess so," said Tamara.

"Would you like a lick or two?" asked Noah.

"No, but I'll sit and watch you lick," said Tamara.

Tamara brushed off the place beside Noah and sat down. "How's the campaign coming?" she asked.

"Fine," said Noah, and he licked.

"Anything new?" asked Tamara. "Since yesterday?"

"No," said Noah.

"Well, what's the latest plan?"

"Nothing to speak of," said Noah.

"You mean you're not going to do anything else to get Maggie elected?"

"I'm doing a very great deal," said Noah. "I'm sitting on a park bench licking a Popsicle. It's an extraordinarily pleasant way to pass time."

Tamara stood up. "Our dear, dear, dear friend Maggie is running for class president and her campaign manager is sitting and licking."

"Actually I am doing something," said Noah. "I'm keeping Maggie away from, uh, complications."

"Complications?" Tamara sat down.

"Well, I believe that Maggie will win by simply using a slogan, posters and a campaign song. I don't want her to get involved in certain, uh, activities."

"Such as?"

"Oh, I don't know."

"Of course you know," said Tamara. "You always know whatever there is to know."

"Well, I do know that sometimes an activity such as, well, for example, a debate could be disastrous."

"Really? I think Maggie would put her very

heart and her very soul and especially her very mouth into a debate," said Tamara.

"Yes, I agree that she would make all those investments," said Noah. "But right now I believe that Maggie is the leading candidate, and, uh, well . . ."

"And you think a debate could spoil that?" asked Tamara.

"I didn't say that," said Noah. "Are you certain you wouldn't care for a last lick before the Popsicle's gone?"

"No, I really have to dash along," said Tamara, getting up.

"Yes, of course," said Noah.

Noah took a long last lick. Then he ate the Popsicle quickly and walked back to school. He felt like whistling, so he did.

He went to Mr. Krickleman's room. Mr. Krickleman was going over some papers.

"Mr. Krickleman?"

"Yes? Oh, hello there, Noah. What can I do for you? *You* don't need any after-school help with your work."

"Well, in a way I need some help," said Noah. "I'd like permission to use the auditorium one afternoon for a debate among presidential candidates."

Mr. Krickleman shot up from his chair. "Of course! Of course! What a worthy cause. What a magnificent utilization of the auditorium. A setting for history, for civics, for statesmanship, that's what an auditorium is all about!"

"Then it's agreeable to you?" said Noah.

"It's more than agreeable," said Mr. Krickleman. "It's perfect."

Noah left the school, whistling again. He had been quite sure his request would be granted. He knew that Mr. Krickleman felt that the English teachers hogged the auditorium for plays.

When Noah got home, he dialed Maggie's number immediately.

Mrs. Marmelstein answered the telephone.

"The digging is done, Mrs. Marmelstein," said Noah. "And I have emerged unscathed."

"I'm glad, Noah," said Mrs. Marmelstein, "and I'll tell Maggie as soon as she gets home."

"Very good. I must hang up now. I have very sticky fingers."

Maggie walked into the kitchen as her mother hung up.

"Maggie," said Mrs. Marmelstein. "Noah just called. He said the digging is done and he is unscathed but very sticky."

The telephone rang again.

Mrs. Marmelstein picked up the receiver.

"So soon you're not sticky?" she said.

"What?" said the voice on the other end.

"This isn't Noah?" said Mrs. Marmelstein.

"This is Thad Smith," said the voice. "Is Maggie there, please?"

"Oh, Thad Smith. Hello there, Thad Smith. Maggie's here. I'm handing her the telephone."

Maggie took the receiver. "Hello, Thad," she said.

"Maggie Marmelstein," said Thad, "I challenge you to a debate."

"Tamara works fast," thought Maggie. "Fast, fast, fast."

"I will debate you anywhere," said Thad. "In the school auditorium. Or in the gym. Or in the lunchroom. I will debate you in the park under the green and fluffy trees. Or in the playground. The laundry room. Name the place. Name the time."

Maggie gasped. She said, "I'll be naming," and she hung up. Where were Thad's cracking voice, knocking knees, and *click-click* teeth?

Maggie knew where. She had them.

11

A Scared Candidate Is a Sunk Candidate

Maggie called Noah.

"Noah," she said, "Thad *wants* to debate me. Anywhere. Anytime. And he means it. I can tell by his voice. Nothing cracks. Nothing *click-clicks*. Noah, I'm scared."

"Listen to me," said Noah. "Maggie Marmelstein doesn't scare. Remember that. A scared candidate is a sunk candidate. *I* feel optimistic. Our plan worked."

Some of Maggie's confidence came back. "So where should we hold the debate?" she asked. "Thad said to name the place."

"In the auditorium," said Noah. "Where you feel at home and Thad feels nervous. I'll set up a time with Thad's campaign manager."

"Henry?"

"Who else? Meanwhile, don't talk to anyone you can't trust."

"I won't. Just old friends. 'Bye, Noah."

Maggie went to her room. She looked at the pictures on her walls. "Fellas, why am I so scared?"

Maggie waited for an answer. "Are you my old friends or not? Answer me why I'm so scared."

"Because of the debate."

"Is that a true answer?"

"Yes, it's a true answer. But it's not a true question."

"The true question is, why do I feel so awful?"

Maggie went up to a picture. "Steve McQueen, I feel awful because Thad is friends with Tamara and she's phony, phony, phony."

Then Maggie spoke to her entire wall. "I just take back what I told Steve McQueen. I don't care at all if Thad likes Tamara. Likes! Likes! Likes!"

The next day at school Maggie watched Thad whenever she could. "It's my job to watch him," she told herself. "I wouldn't bother to watch him if it weren't my job. I wouldn't pay any attention to him at all."

And Maggie watched Tamara, too. Maggie watched Thad and Tamara separately and she watched them together. She hated their having the same first initial. She hated their having the same color hair. She hated the conversation they were having now beside a water fountain and under a poster that had just been put up: DON'T BE DRAGGY, VOTE FOR MAGGIE!

Tamara was smiling at Thad. Thad was smiling at Tamara.

"Why should Thad like a spy when he doesn't like me?" Maggie asked herself. She asked herself the same question all morning.

Suddenly Maggie felt sick. "Maybe it's a virus," she thought. "I can't get sick now that I'm running for president. But maybe if I have to stay out of school a lot, Thad Smith will worry. Down deep, Thad Smith will worry."

When lunchtime came, Maggie didn't feel like eating. She walked home and went straight to bed.

12

Special Delivery

"You're nuts to do this," Henry said to Thad as they walked home from school that afternoon.

Thad stopped walking. "You're supposed to be my campaign manager. You're not supposed to think I'm nuts," he said.

"Well, it's nuts to bring Maggie Marmelstein's homework to her just because she was out sick this afternoon," said Henry. "I mean, she hates you or something, so why do her a favor?"

Thad started to walk again. "She's sick and I figure she needs her homework for the weekend. And she lives right on my floor. I'm taking my own homework home which is the same as her homework, so I'm not really bringing her *her* homework. It's just mine that's the same as hers."

"It's still nuts," said Henry. "Look, the more homework you take to her, the smarter she'll get, and the smarter she gets, the harder it will be to win over her for president. Bet you didn't think of that. That's what a manager's for. To think of that."

"The homework is just a composition about a cow or a train or a family or an earthquake. And five apples-and-pears problems. Nothing there to help her become president."

"Maggie will find something," said Henry.

"Are you joking?"

"No."

"You used to make jokes, Henry, but you don't anymore. And now I need them. You could write me a speech with jokes. When a candidate makes kids laugh, sometimes they like him more."

"I'll make jokes after you win," said Henry.

"Being president will be big stuff, Henry. The biggest stuff. The second that Mr. Krickleman told us about the idea, I knew I wanted to be that big stuff, the president. Up to now, I haven't been any kind of stuff."

"Last year you were frog stuff in the class play," said Henry.

"Don't remind me," said Thad.

"Well, you have to get rid of your frog image," said Henry. "Did you notice that in all the work I've done for your campaign, I haven't written or mentioned frog or croak or pond or green? I've kept away from all of that."

Thad and Henry stopped in front of Thad's apartment house. "Here's where you deliver your cow," said Henry. "See you tomorrow."

Thad went up to his floor and down the hall to Apartment 2B. He rang the bell. Mrs. Marmelstein answered. She smiled. "My frog friend and presidential candidate, Thad Smith. Hello."

"Hello," said Thad. "I brought Maggie's homework. Is she still sick?"

"She's on the border line," said Mrs. Marmelstein. "She's too sick to go to school, but too well to stay home. Soon she'll cross the border one way or the other. Would you like to come in and have some leftover victory cake?"

"Whose victory?"

"I made it for Maggie, but the piece you eat you can pretend it's anything you want it to be."

"I'm not hungry right now," said Thad. "Not for *Maggie's* victory cake," he thought. "Not for one bite. Not for one nibble. Not for one crumb."

"Some other time then," said Mrs. Marmelstein. "Thank you for the homework. Maggie will thank you in person when she's better."

"Well, she doesn't have to," said Thad, "unless she wants to."

He walked down the hall to his apartment.

Mrs. Marmelstein opened the door of Maggie's

bedroom very quietly and peeked inside. "Awake? Oh, good. Your homework's here. Special delivery."

Maggie sat up in bed. "Who delivered it special?" she asked.

"Thad Smith."

"Thad Smith?"

"Yes, Thad Smith. You never heard of him? Ex-frog, present presidential candidate, neighbor, fellow student, and now homework special deliverer?"

"Why did he do that?"

"So you could have your homework," said Mrs. Marmelstein. "Wasn't that nice of him?"

"I'm suspicious," said Maggie.

"Suspicious? That's not good," said Mrs. Marmelstein. "He delivered it special."

Maggie got out of bed. "I'm feeling much better now," she said.

"Well, let's wait for perfect," said Mrs. Marmelstein. "And bed is the best place to wait."

Maggie looked down at her slippers. "Okay," she sighed. "I guess I'll have to wait." Maggie climbed back into bed. "Anyway," she said, "I want to be perfect for Monday. What did Thad say when he brought my homework?"

"He said, 'I brought Maggie's homework,'" said Mrs. Marmelstein.

"Did he say anything else?"

"Yes, he asked if you were still sick."

"He did? How did he ask it?"

"Well, the usual way. With words and feeling," said Mrs. Marmelstein.

"Feeling?"

"Yes."

"Like he cared?"

"Like he cared."

Maggie smoothed her blankets. "Now that I'm a presidential candidate I like to get all the facts," she said.

13

Signed, A Friend

When Maggie got up on Monday she felt very good.

Mrs. Marmelstein looked at her. "You crossed the border," she said, "into the right territory."

"Yes, I feel terrific today," said Maggie. "You know, I feel so good that when I get to be president I might not make Thad Smith the blackboard eraser person after all."

"What's that?" asked Mrs. Marmelstein.

Maggie shrugged. "If Thad Smith can do me a favor, I can do him a favor."

When Maggie got to school, she looked for Thad before her first class. She wanted to thank him for bringing her homework. But she didn't see him. She looked for him after class. But he was busy talking with Tamara.

"Talk, talk, talk," thought Maggie. "Phony talk, talk, talk. That's all Tamara knows how to do. Thad will find that out. He will. He has to."

All through the school day Maggie looked for a chance to see Thad alone. "I'll wait until after school," she finally decided. "At home, at the apartment house, that's the best."

When Maggie got home from school, Mrs. Marmelstein was waving an envelope in the air. "Mail for Maggie Marmelstein," she said.

She handed Maggie the envelope. Maggie opened it quickly. She pulled a piece of paper from it and read it.

"From maybe Cary Grant?" asked Mrs. Marmelstein.

"No!" said Maggie. "From maybe Thad and Tamara. No wonder they had plenty to talk about. I hate them! I hate them! But I hate Thad the most because I almost liked him."

Maggie handed the paper to her mother.

Mrs. Marmelstein read it out loud.

THE SIXTH GRADE NEEDS
MAGGIE MARMELSTEIN LIKE
a fatal disease
a room full of fleas
an elephant's sneeze
a wart on their nose
a rip in their clothes
a spike in their bed
a hole in their head
Signed, A Friend

14

"I Never Mailed You Anything!"

"Oh dear," said Mrs. Marmelstein. "Even in a democracy a note like this should be against the law. And who is 'A Friend' with no name? A no-name friend is no friend."

"Thad and Tamara!" said Maggie. "I just know it's from them."

"Anonymous is who it's from," said Mrs. Marmelstein. "And the garbage pail is its natural destination. Drop it in. Make it disappear."

She handed the paper back to Maggie.

Suddenly Maggie turned and ran out of the apartment and down the hall. She stopped at 2D and knocked on the door. No one answered. She ran down to the laundry room. It was empty. She ran outside. She saw Thad Smith sitting against a wall, reading a book.

Maggie ran up to him. She held the piece of paper and the envelope in front of his face. "This," she said, "is a dirty trick."

Thad closed his book. "Is that your grocery list?" he asked.

"Oh sure," said Maggie. "An elephant's sneeze, a wart, a spike. Don't pretend you don't know about it. Don't pretend that you and Tamara didn't write this and mail it to me."

"We didn't," said Thad. "Whatever it is. I never mailed you anything in my life."

"Yes, you did. You even signed your name to something once."

"To what?"

"Don't you remember?"

"Remember what?"

"Nothing."

"Tell me."

"Okay. I'll tell you to prove that you sent it," said Maggie. "It was mostly colored red and it had a picture of a little house, and in each little window of the little house there was a message."

"I don't send messages in little windows of little houses," said Thad. "That's dumb."

"Well, you sent it to me."

"When?"

"In the third grade. In February. In just about the middle of the month."

"Oh *then*," said Thad. "How come you still remember, then?"

"I don't," said Maggie. "But I own some stuff that I forgot to throw away and that's one of them. I have a sea horse made of yarn that I forgot to throw away. And some little plastic faces that you can stick on the ends of shoelaces. And a picture of Ellen's goldfish that came out blue. I have lots of things that I forgot to throw away. And I'm going inside right now and throw away your house thing and this horrible thing you just sent me."

"I said I didn't send that horrible thing."

"How do you know it's a horrible thing?"

"You just said it was."

"Thad Smith, you are going to be sorry you sent this. Just wait until our debate."

"I can hardly wait," said Thad.

Maggie tore up the paper and the envelope. The pieces dropped at Thad's feet.

"Litterer!" he said.

"It's your paper. I'm just giving it back," said Maggie.

She turned and went back into the house. When she got to her room, she knelt down and pulled a large box out from under her bed. It had MAG-GIE MARMELSTEIN, PRIVATE printed across the top. Maggie opened the box and started to look through the papers inside. She pulled something out of the box. An old valentine in the shape of a

house. All the windows in the house were shaped like hearts. The valentine was signed FROM THAD SMITH. Maggie took the valentine to the wastebasket. She held it by one corner over the basket. She held it there for a long time. Then she took the valentine back to the box and put it inside. She closed the box and put it under her bed.

15

"I Don't Believe You!"

Henry was drinking from a water fountain.

"Hello, Henry," said Noah, coming up behind him.

Henry kept drinking.

"I'm right here, Henry. Behind you. Waiting for you until you're not thirsty anymore."

Henry kept drinking.

"Henry!" said Noah.

"I don't think I'm supposed to talk to you, Noah," said Henry, wiping his mouth. "So don't talk to me so I won't have to not talk to you on purpose."

"Why?"

"Aren't campaign managers for rival candidates not supposed to talk to each other?" asked Henry. "Aren't we enemies or something like that?"

"No," said Noah.

"I'd rather be enemies and not talk to you until the election is over," said Henry. "There's something about you since you became Maggie's manager, something about the way you walk, something about the way your head comes out at an angle from your neck, something about you that's *different*. So couldn't you, like, *save* whatever you have to say until after the election?"

"I just wanted to set up a time for the debate between Maggie and Thad. That's all," said Noah.

"Why don't Maggie and Thad decide?" asked Henry.

"Because it's our job. Yours and mine."

"Ours, huh?"

"Yes, and I suggest we hold the debate the day before the election. So it will be fresh in everybody's mind when they vote."

"Well, I've got a system worked out for this campaign," said Henry. "Bet you didn't know that, Noah. Well, it's a great system and you can't beat it. And I have to consult the system before I can give you my answer."

"How long will it take?" asked Noah.

"Just a few minutes," said Henry. "I need a piece of paper, a crossword puzzle, two paper clips and this incantation that I keep in my pocket. I have everything right here. Do you mind turning your back to me?"

"Is this system based on the supernatural?" asked Noah, turning his back.

"Do you think I'm nutty?" said Henry. "This is scientific and it's mine alone. Please be silent for one minute."

Noah kept quiet.

At last Henry said, "The system says to hold the debate in seven days."

"That's the day before the election," said Noah. "So we agree."

"We agree," said Henry.

"On what?" asked Thad Smith, who had just walked up to the fountain.

"On when to hold the debate," said Henry. "In seven days."

"Okay," said Thad. "I'll go tell Maggie right now."

"Noah can tell her," said Henry.

"Well, I can because I'll be right near where she is," said Thad.

"Where's that?" asked Henry.

"It's where she is," said Thad.

"Maggie's in the office waiting for a permission slip," said Noah.

"That's just where I was going to be right near," said Thad. "The office."

"But . . ." said Henry.

Thad walked off. He went to the school office.

He saw Maggie sitting there on a bench. He sat down beside her. "I've got news," he said.

"Oh?" said Maggie. "In rhyme?"

"I came to tell you that the debate will be in seven days," said Thad. "I walked down two corridors and past fourteen doors just to tell you that."

"Why?"

"Because that proves I didn't send that note because by the time I get back to where I started from at the water fountain I'll have walked down four corridors and past twenty-eight doors just to tell you when the debate is. A person who sent that note wouldn't have done that. Not four corridors, not twenty-eight doors."

"I don't believe you," said Maggie. "I wouldn't believe you even if it was one hundred corridors and one thousand doors and a climb up a mountain and a hike across the country. That's how far I wouldn't believe you."

Maggie got up and walked out of the office. She forgot all about her permission slip.

16

Terrible Terrible Trouble

MARMELS-TEAM was hard at work, at school and at home, making more and more posters, writing new slogans, finishing the song and trying to get their friends to vote for Maggie. Maggie felt funny whenever she looked at the posters of herself and Thad and the other four candidates hanging around the halls of the school. She only looked at them when she thought no one was watching her.

In the art room, Dipsey Ford and Jody Klinger were drawing a new poster, with the face of each candidate except Maggie over the picture of a big drum. The poster read:

THE ONLY ONE
WHO CAN'T BE BEAT—
MAGGIE MARMELSTEIN!!

Dipsey and Jody were arguing over how many exclamation marks there should be. Dipsey wanted three. "Two's plenty, three's a crowd," Jody said.

She had heard a saying like that somewhere. "Let's take a vote," she said. "We'll stand in the doorway and ask kids as they go by how many exclamation marks there should be. They can vote for three or two. Okay?"

"Okay," said Dipsey.

As kids walked by, Jody and Dipsey yelled, waved, signaled and pulled them over to the poster. "Vote for two or three exclamation marks," they said.

Soon they were surrounded by kids. Some laughed, some mumbled, but all were curious. Only four were willing to vote, and it was a tie.

Maggie came along. "What's going on?" she asked.

A lot of kids clapped.

"Hooray, it's Maggie Marmelstein," said Mitchell Fritz. "She'll solve the problem. A candidate for president has a solution for everything."

"What do you want me to solve?" asked Maggie. She felt suddenly nervous. So many kids seemed to be waiting for her to supply some kind of magic. And she saw Thad coming along with Tamara to watch.

"*You* decide whether there should be two or three exclamation marks after MAGGIE MARMELSTEIN on this poster," said Jody. "I say two, Dipsey says three."

Maggie knew that if she answered three, she would lose Jody. If she answered two, she would lose Dipsey. Either way she would lose the confidence the kids had that she would come up with a special solution.

"Maggie Marmelstein, you seem to be in terrible, terrible, terrible trouble," said Tamara, grinning. "Is there anything I can do to help?"

"Don't rush me," said Maggie. "I'm going to tell all of you just how to solve the problem." Maggie remembered how Thad had been stuck for something to say in front of a group. But he hadn't had a puzzle to solve. Maggie looked at Thad. He looked sad.

Maggie saw Noah at the back of the group. He started to move quickly toward her. As he moved he said, "Come, let's all of us disband immediately. I believe we're in violation of the fire laws."

"Since when?" said Ronald. "Since Maggie's stuck for an answer?"

"Tell, tell, tell," said Tamara.

Maggie looked at Noah.

Noah announced, "This exclamation-mark problem is not a suitable one to claim the time and attention of a presidential candidate. Jody and Dipsey are both right. Jody is right in wanting to have two exclamation marks on this poster, and Dipsey is right in not wanting to leave out an exclamation mark. Therefore we will not use the third exclamation mark on this poster, but we will use it on the DON'T BE DRAGGY, VOTE FOR MAGGIE! poster after the word MAGGIE, which currently has only one exclamation mark."

Everyone clapped, including three teachers.

"You were terrific, Noah," said Maggie.

"Noah's terrific," someone else said. "Noah would make a terrific president."

"Definitely," said someone else.

Maggie looked at Noah closely. Noah *would* make a terrific president. But he didn't want to be president. Maybe *she* didn't want to be president either. What was it all about anyway, being president? Well, she wasn't going to quit now. Not with the chance to debate Thad Smith, not with the chance to get even with him.

Thad and Tamara were standing a few feet away. They hadn't moved, and their faces hadn't moved. Thad still looked sad, and Tamara was still grinning.

Maggie walked past them very fast. Noah followed.

17

Mean Against Maggie

"Is the library closed?" Noah asked Mrs. Bromley as he stood at the entrance. "Nobody's here but us."

"No, it's just a quiet time," said Mrs. Bromley.

Noah stepped into the room. "I like quiet times," he said. "Occasionally when I take a bus I'm the only passenger on it, and that's a quiet time. The driver and I are sort of like partners in a quiet adventure. And this quiet library, that's another adventure. Just you and I and all these books."

"I know exactly what you mean," said Mrs. Bromley. "Tell me, can I help you with today's adventure?"

"Today I'm meeting Maggie Marmelstein here to discuss our strategy for the debate. But you could help me with a problem. I said something in public yesterday concerning exclamation marks that has caused five different kids to say 'Hooray for Noah' five different times as I walked by. I also heard 'Cheers!' twice, 'Noah's the greatest' four times and I got slapped on the back once in a friendly way."

"That all sounds quite enthusiastic, Noah. I don't think it's a problem."

"Well, out of context it isn't, but in context it is." Noah looked toward the door. "Here comes Maggie. I'll talk to you again."

"Anytime, Noah."

Noah and Maggie went to their usual place in the library and sat down. "The debate is less than a week away," said Noah. "Let's discuss what you want to say, what points you want to stress, what promises, if any, you want to make."

"Points and promises don't count," said Maggie. "They're nothing. I've got important things to say, and I don't have to rehearse or plan them."

Noah frowned. "Maggie," he whispered, "you don't seem scared anymore. You seem mad. Furious. Has something happened concerning Thad that you haven't told me about?"

"Yes."

"Tell me, so I can help."

"It was something mean, Noah. Something mean and anonymous."

"Let me help you with mean and anonymous," whispered Noah. "We'll tackle it together."

"No, this was mean against me. Me, Maggie Marmelstein. It was like the meanness was saved up and then when I became a candidate, they wrote it down and sent it to me. And I have to take care of it myself."

"Now *I'm* scared," said Noah. "Scared about what you'll do and say."

"I'm not," said Maggie. "I'll win that debate. I'll win big. As big as—"

"As what?" asked Noah.

"An elephant's sneeze," said Maggie. "That's how big."

18

"Boo to You, Too!"

Five kids had left MARMELS-TEAM, but three others had joined. Noah had said that there were always "professional joiners and leavers" in a campaign, and that they should be allowed to join and leave without question.

Ronald the Rock Thrower, who hadn't joined any group, stood up and announced his own candidacy in the lunchroom. Ralph then got up and said, "Anybody who votes for Ronald has rocks in his head." Ralph was cheered. Somebody threw him a big bag of miniature marshmallows. He gave a mock bow, sat down, opened the bag and had a feast. Ronald stood up again. "Give me some goodies and I won't run for president," he said.

"That's blackmail," said Mitchell Fritz.

"That's a good idea," said Cynthia Stauffeur. "It's worth my spice cake with raisins, cherry bits and cloves."

"It's worth half my peach. That's all," said Henry, biting into his peach.

Noah got up. "The only reason for becoming a candidate," he said, "is a deep desire to do something for the sixth grade. Candidacies should not be bought—or eaten."

"Hey, you got something there, Noah," said Ronald. "I'm already doing a lot for the sixth grade just by being in it."

"Boo," said an entire row of kids. "Down with Ronald."

"Boo to you, too," said Ronald. "Just for that I'm not running."

"Hooray! Hooray!" Applause. Whistles.

Ronald looked at Maggie, Thad and the four other candidates. "Did you hear that?" he said. "Unanimous applause and cheers. *U-nan-i-mous!* None of you ever got unanimous, did you? *I* can *unite* the sixth grade. I have *already* united the sixth grade. That's doing something for the sixth grade, isn't it, Noah?"

"Well, in a way, yes," said Noah.

"Noah agrees. And I think I've already done too much for the sixth grade. So I'll accept all contributions, including a spice cake with raisins, cherry bits and cloves, from the grateful."

"I ate it up when Noah said that candidacies shouldn't be eaten," said Cynthia.

90

"Here's three quarters of a peach," said Henry. "I always was a sport."

During the last days of the campaign, the sixth grade continued to divide into two strong camps: the Maggie camp and the Thad camp. The other four candidates were slowly dropping out. One quit, saying, "Who wants to be president, anyway? That's a dumb job." Two other candidates were eliminated when they were discovered trying to sell secret combination numbers of gym lockers. The last candidate was eliminated when he was caught trying to buy one.

"The election is now between you and Thad Smith," Noah announced the day before the debate. "The last candidate is out."

"Terrific," said Maggie. "That's just the way I wanted it."

Noah looked straight at Maggie. "Maggie, what do you want more?" he asked. "To be president? Or to beat Thad Smith?"

Maggie didn't answer.

19

The Great Debate

It was the day of the debate.

Maggie was not hungry for breakfast.

"Presidents, future presidents, ambassadors, emperors, dukes, duchesses and citizens everywhere eat breakfast," said Mrs. Marmelstein. "You, Madam Future President of the Sixth Grade, don't have to eat a big breakfast or even a medium-sized breakfast. Just put something in your mouth so your stomach will know you didn't forget about it. Just a little token of remembrance. That's all."

Maggie ate half a waffle and drank some orange juice. Then she got her books together for school. Her mother kissed her good-bye. "That's a presidential kiss," said Mrs. Marmelstein. "I wish they'd let me watch the presidential debate. I wouldn't be a bother. I would cheer you in peace and quiet inside me where no one could hear."

"No parents or teachers are allowed," said

Maggie. "Except for Mr. Krickleman, our social studies teacher. He has to come to make sure we do things right."

Maggie started to walk to school. She heard someone in back of her trying to catch up. It was Ronald. "I wish you luck today," he said. "But I'm not saying what kind."

"Funny, funny," said Maggie. Up ahead she saw someone who was hoping very hard that Maggie would win. It was Ellen.

"Oh, Maggie, don't listen to anything Ronald says, whatever it is," said Ellen. "When you get to be president of the sixth grade, you'll be president of Ronald, too, won't you? Then maybe he'll act nicer. I'm going to try to sit in the front row at the debate, but if I can't, then I'll sit in the second row. And if I can't do that, I'll sit in the third row. If you can't see me, I'll still be there and I want you to think of me as being there."

"Oh, Ellen, I will," said Maggie.

Maggie and Ellen walked on silently. When they got to school, they saw Thad, Tamara and Henry talking together near the entrance.

Ellen whispered, "They scare me. Standing together like that. Like they've got the power or something. Don't they scare you?"

"No!" said a voice behind them. It was Noah. "Thad, Tamara and Henry are simply three human beings of juvenile age who are standing and talking together in front of a school," said Noah. "I see no evidence of great power and no cause for alarm."

"Boy, Noah, I sure know why you're Maggie's manager," said Ellen. "You used to be like me, didn't you? Kind of a way-in-back kid. And now you're like—*you*. You're a really front-row person now, Noah."

"Thank you, Ellen. But you're definitely tops just the way you are. Whenever I see you, I know I can expect a friendly greeting, an honest smile, kind words and excellent intentions. I hope that throughout my life I will be surrounded by people with such fine qualities."

"Marry Ellen and you can be sure of it!" said Maggie.

Ellen looked at her shoes.

Noah looked at Ellen's shoes.

Maggie knew that Ellen and Noah were still alike in some important ways.

School started. Maggie tried hard to concentrate on her work. But she couldn't. Every time she passed a Maggie poster in the hallway she felt that she was on top and that a strong, actually invincible MARMELS-TEAM was backing her up. Then she would glance at a Thad poster and admit to herself that he had a good group working for him, too. Thoughts of power and glory and defeat and spikes and warts and a house-shaped valentine and victory cake and green and fluffy trees and a dripping ice-cream cone went through her head in no particular order.

"Here we go," said Noah.

The last bell had sounded, and school was over for the day. It was time to go to the auditorium for the debate. Anybody in the sixth grade who wanted to see the debate could walk in and see it. Maggie, Noah and Ellen walked together. Maggie and Noah went to the stage, where four chairs had been placed. Maggie sat on an outer chair and Noah sat beside her. Thad and Henry came up and sat on the other two chairs. Thad took the outer chair, the one farthest from Maggie.

Mr. Krickleman walked in, surrounded by a lot of sixth graders who were asking him questions. He was happy about this opportunity to show the sixth grade how a political debate worked.

Finally everyone was seated. Almost all of the sixth grade had come. Maggie saw Tamara in the front row. A few members of MARMELS-TEAM —Ralph, Jody, Mitchell and Dipsey—were also sitting in the front row. Ellen was in the second row. Mr. Krickleman sat on the piano bench just below the stage.

Suddenly Maggie didn't feel at home on the

stage. She felt she was on a battleground.

Mr. Krickleman rose and said, "Members of the sixth grade, this afternoon we will hear a debate between the two candidates for the office of class president: Maggie Marmelstein and Thad Smith. They will be introduced by their campaign managers: Noah Moore for Maggie and Henry Emery for Thad."

Suddenly Ralph and Jody stood up. Ralph was holding his guitar, which he had just taken out of its case. He stuck a collapsible cowboy hat, which he had swiftly removed from his pocket and opened, onto his head. He started to play and sing:

> *Well, I'm walkin' down a lonely road,*
> *And I'm cryin' in a dream,*
> *And I'm needin' help with problems,*
> *And I think of Marmelstein.*
>
> *'Cause I'm tired of walkin' lonely,*
> *And I'm tired of cryin', too.*
> *So I'm askin' Maggie Marmelstein*
> *To see what she can do.*

Henry got up from his chair, almost knocking it over. "I object!" he said. "This is a debate, not a musical show. I know at least six people who can sing and dance for Thad Smith. And do imitations, too, and one can juggle three Frisbees at a time and one can play songs with a spoon and a glass. And I want equal time for them to do their thing for Thad Smith."

Mr. Krickleman spoke. "Henry is right to object. However, since the song did not deal with any issues, it won't affect the debate. But, just to be completely fair, after the debate anyone wishing to perform in behalf of Thad Smith is entitled to three minutes. Now, will the campaign managers please introduce their candidates. Henry, as long as you are on your feet, you may go first."

Henry walked to the center of the stage. "Thad Smith is," he said.

There was a long pause.

"Is Thad Smith," Henry continued. "And who is Thad Smith? He's a great guy. The first time I ever saw this great guy, I said to myself, 'This is a great guy.' Everything about him right away was great. All great. All right away. And when somebody is a great guy, what else can I say about him except one word: president. When I look at Thad, this great guy, I think President Smith. *President* Thad Smith. That sounds right to me. Doesn't that sound right to you?"

A few kids in the audience yelled at the same time, "Right!" "Wrong!" "Right!" "Wrong!"

Henry went on. "I now introduce a great guy, our future president, Thad Smith!"

There was some applause and whistling.

Thad stood up, waved and sat down.

Noah got up and walked to the center of the stage.

"My fellow sixth graders," he said, "this election is not a popularity contest. The president of the sixth grade should be chosen on the basis of what *she*—or he—can do for the sixth grade. Is everybody in the sixth grade happy?"

"NO!" some kids shouted.

"Could life be better in the sixth grade? Do we need changes? Can we improve the way things are done?"

"Yes, yes, yes!" cried the audience.

"The sixth grade needs help," said Noah. "And my candidate, Maggie Marmelstein, will help the sixth grade. And here she is—my candidate and yours—Maggie Marmelstein!"

There was some applause and whistling. Maggie couldn't tell whether there was more or less than for Thad.

Maggie stood up, waved and sat down.

Mr. Krickleman said, "We will now flip a coin to see which candidate speaks first." He held up a nickel. "Heads or tails?" he asked.

"Heads," said Maggie and Thad.

Everyone laughed and clapped.

Noah said, "My candidate is willing to speak first *or* second. It's the words and not their order that's important."

Thad stood up. "I'll let Maggie go first or second."

"No special favors," said Maggie. "I can win on my own."

Mr. Krickleman said, "Will one of you please start the debate."

Maggie stood up. "I should be president because I'll be a better president than Thad Smith, who sometimes isn't very good at all, especially in his WRITTEN WORK."

"Please be careful of character assassination, Maggie," said Mr. Krickleman. "Thad, would you care to comment on your written work as pertains to the presidency?"

"Yes, I would care to comment on that," said Thad. "On that very thing, my written work. In that very way that you mentioned. Yes, I would. Well, my written work is, um, splendiferous."

"What's that?" said someone in the audience. "Wow!"

"Big words. I don't use big words," said Maggie. "Why, I've got a campaign manager, Noah, who knows more big words than every kid in this room put together. But I wouldn't borrow any big words, because a presidential candidate shouldn't be a borrower of words or anything."

Thad spoke. "Well, all I borrow are pencils, and money for the ice-cream machine. I'll be a good president."

"Why?" asked Mr. Krickleman. "Discuss the issues, please."

"So will I," said Maggie.

"Issues, issues," said Mr. Krickleman.

"I'll be better than you," said Maggie.

"No, I'll be better than you," said Thad.

"ISSUES! ISSUES!" called Mr. Krickleman.

"I will be a fair and honest president," said Maggie.

"I will be a fair and honest president," said Thad.

"Details, details," called Mr. Krickleman.

Maggie turned to Thad. "*You're* fair and honest?" she yelled.

Noah, who had sat down, stood up. "Members of the sixth grade, Maggie Marmelstein is planning many exciting and worthwhile projects for the sixth grade. For example, a monthly newspaper, a class picnic in the spring—"

"Who sez? You sez or she sez?" yelled Ronald. "If she sez, let her say!"

Noah turned to Maggie. "Maggie?"

But Maggie was still looking at Thad. "*You're* fair and honest?" she repeated. "Sending a crummy note with no name signed to a candidate isn't fair *or* honest!"

"I didn't send that crummy note," said Thad.

Maggie walked up to Thad and looked straight at him. "You sent it because you thought I was winning and you were trying to get me to lose. Do you think a note like that would make me quit?"

Noah went over to Maggie and whispered, "What note? What note? Is this what you couldn't tell me?"

Mr. Krickleman spoke. "I think we've explored this note business as far as we should at this time. Could you please go on to another, more relevant topic."

Tamara stood up. "I think this is a marvelous topic. Maggie has accused Thad of writing a bad note. If the note was that bad, we should *see* it. The sixth grade should have the evidence."

Maggie looked at all the faces in the audience. Faces waiting for her to say something. And the most awful face of all: Tamara's. It was smiling the most rotten smile Maggie had ever seen.

"I tore the note up," Maggie said at last.

"Tore it up?" said Tamara. "Tore up evidence

like that! How do we know there even *was* a note?"

Somebody yelled, "Let's hear it for Thad Smith!"

Maggie wanted to cry. She had lost. Unfairly. She did not want to win unfairly or lose unfairly.

Suddenly Thad Smith shouted, "*I* saw the note. Maggie tore it up and I put it back together with Scotch tape. And I read it. And it was crummy."

Then Thad shouted louder. "Tamara Axelrod, *you* knew about the note. I *told* you about it. And I told you Maggie tore it up."

Everyone looked at Tamara.

"Confess!" yelled Ronald.

"Oh, shut up, Ronald," said Tamara. Then she turned to face the class. "So what if I wrote that note?" she said. "It was a glorious note. Glorious, glorious, glorious."

"It was crummy, crummy, crummy," said Thad Smith.

Tamara turned and stared at Thad. "I worked hard for your campaign, Thad Smith," she said.

"How hard?" asked Thad.

"Harder than you know about."

"Zowie!" thought Maggie. "Thad didn't even know she was snooping for him. Tamara was a self-employed spy."

"I told you to keep your eyes and ears open.

That's all," said Thad. He spoke louder. "That's fair and honest, class. I am a fair and honest candidate."

"In addition to being great," yelled Henry.

Now Mr. Krickleman was yelling. "Order! Order! The debate is over!"

"Wait!" yelled Henry. "You owe us three minutes to sing a Thad Smith song."

"Very well. Quickly a Thad Smith song," said Mr. Krickleman.

"We didn't bring a song," said Henry. "Is a cheer okay?"

"Very well. A cheer. A *quick* cheer," said Mr. Krickleman.

Henry raised his arms. "T is for terrific. H is for honest. A is for A great guy. D is for—for—"

"Defeat!" yelled Ronald.

Some of the class yelled "boo" and some of the class yelled "yay."

Mr. Krickleman hustled the class out of the auditorium.

Maggie, Noah, Thad and Henry stood silently on the stage looking at one another. Maggie did not know what to say to anybody. Everything had happened so fast. She had accused Thad of something he hadn't done. But instead of getting revenge, he had saved her chance to be president. And he had told off Tamara.

Maggie held out her hand in Thad's direction. "Good luck," she said, "to a good opponent."

Thad shook her hand. "Good luck to you, too," he said.

Henry shrugged his shoulders. He held out his hand to Noah. "Good luck, Noah," he said.

"Good luck to you, Henry," said Noah.

Maggie, Noah, Thad and Henry left the stage.

20

"I Want To Tell You Something."

Maggie ran home. She had to tell her mother what had happened.

Mrs. Marmelstein was mixing a victory cake. "For tomorrow," she said, as Maggie walked in. "When your victory is fresh, and the cake isn't. Sometimes it tastes better the second day." Then Mrs. Marmelstein said, "The debate. What happened at the debate? Who won? I'm looking at your face, but your face isn't looking one way or the other. Last night on *The Late Late Show* there was an inspector who solved his cases by looking at people's faces. He would have lost your case."

"Well," said Maggie, "nobody won. The debate kind of blew up."

"An explosion?"

"Well, a lot of words exploded," said Maggie, "and I started it."

Maggie sat down at the kitchen table. She told her mother what had happened. When Maggie was finished, her mother said, "Thad Smith rescued you."

"Yeah," said Maggie.

"What's the matter? You didn't want to be rescued?" asked Mrs. Marmelstein.

"Not by him," said Maggie. "Now I'm trying to beat somebody who could have won over me today and didn't. Running for president is very confusing."

Mrs. Marmelstein stuck her mixing spoon into the mixture in her bowl and sat down. "Maggie," she said. "Remember when we were making the victory cake last time? You were measuring times four and I was mixing and asking questions."

"I remember," said Maggie. "You asked, Why do you want to be president? When you're president what will you be doing? Can you offer any Maggie specialties?"

"And you said it was hard to explain," said Mrs. Marmelstein. "Well, you don't have to explain it to me. But shouldn't you explain it to yourself?"

Maggie was thinking. What could she explain to herself? That her main reason for running for president was to beat Thad Smith. That she hadn't even thought about what she would *do* as president. She had only thought about what she would *be*. A winner over Thad Smith. Nothing that had anything to do with helping the sixth grade.

Thad, too, had been advertising himself, not his services, not any ideas for helping the sixth grade.

Maggie got up. "I'm taking a little walk," she said.

"Have a good one," said Mrs. Marmelstein. "And be back for supper."

Maggie walked down the stairs to the laundry room. Thad Smith was there with a basket of laundry.

"I'm looking for you," said Maggie. "This is the first place I'm looking."

"How come you thought I'd be here?" asked Thad. "This is the last place you should think I'd be, because as I told you, I come here only a couple of times a year. I'm starting on a new year today and this is my first time for the new year. So that means I will be here only one more time this year. So don't look for me here anymore."

"This is a dopey time to do laundry," said Maggie. "How can you think about dirty clothes when the election is tomorrow?"

"I like it here. Twice a year," said Thad. "Clothes are nice. Dirty clothes are the best. Dirty clothes need help."

"The sixth grade needs help, too," said Maggie. "Did you ever think of that?"

"Is that a trick question?"

"No."

"How come it isn't a trick question when the election is tomorrow?"

"I wouldn't ask you a trick question," said Maggie.

"Well, it might turn out to be a trick question even if it didn't start out to be. Henry warned me about those kinds of questions. And besides, the last time I saw you here, you said *I* needed help. So I'm not answering any help questions. I'll answer questions about the weather, ice-cream sundaes, my stamp collection, newspapers and gerbils. I'll talk about any and all of those subjects."

"Well, I want to tell you something."

"What?"

Maggie bent down and started to sort Thad's laundry into piles.

While she was looking down she said, "Today, Henry said you were great. I don't think you're great."

"I know you don't," said Thad.

Maggie shook out some gravel from a bunched-up stocking. "But I think you're sometimes great," she said. "Okay?"

"Sure," said Thad.

21

"Your New President Is . . ."

Maggie made a small x in the space beside the name *Maggie Marmelstein* on the ballot. She had always planned to make a huge X, but now she didn't feel like it.

Maggie put her ballot through the slot in the ballot box. The box was closely guarded by Mr. Krickleman in his social studies classroom. As each member of the sixth grade voted, Mr. Krickleman crossed a name off his long list. The ballots had the names *Maggie Marmelstein* and *Thad Smith* printed on them, and a third name: *Other*. "Other," Mr. Krickleman had said, "is anyone else in the sixth grade you wish to vote for. Simply write in the name. Please refrain from voting for your dog, your favorite television program, various fruits and vegetables, detergents, musical groups, sports heroes, assorted rodents or any other idea that you think is funny. It might *be* funny, but it will be a wasted vote. Anyone can vote for himself or herself, as Maggie and Thad of course know. There are forty-nine students in the sixth grade. Four are absent today. So we should have forty-five votes."

The name of the winner was to be announced in the lunchroom after school. Mr. Krickleman had scheduled it for the auditorium, but he had canceled after yesterday's debate. "The lunchroom—well, that's always a mess," Maggie had heard him say to another teacher. "But the auditorium will never regain its grasp on serenity if I have one more catastrophe like yesterday's."

Maggie wished the election were over. She tried not to look at Thad during the day. She tried not to look at the campaign posters. She tried to pretend to herself that she wasn't a candidate. "I'm silly," she told herself. "I should be eager, but instead I'm silly."

Ellen and Noah were waiting to walk to the lunchroom with her after school.

"I must tell you," said Noah, "that I think the election will be very close. Nobody won the debate yesterday, because there was, in fact, no debate."

"Well, whatever it was, Tamara lost it," said Ellen.

Maggie smiled. She felt good when Ellen said that. Very good.

"Where should we sit?" asked Maggie when

they reached the lunchroom.

"Anywhere the president wishes," said Noah.

"That table by the window," said Maggie.

"Excellent," said Noah. "A kind of natural spotlight on the winner."

"You think of everything, Noah," said Maggie.

"Well, I've tried to help you win," said Noah. "And in these last few moments before the winner is announced, I want you to know that it's made me thoroughly happy to be your campaign manager."

"We've enjoyed having you, haven't we, Maggie?" said Ellen.

"You're the best, Noah," said Maggie.

Maggie saw Thad and Henry come into the lunchroom. They sat down at the next table. Maggie thought they looked terrific together, just the two of them, like old times. No Tamara. Tamara wasn't anywhere in the room. Maggie wondered if she had even voted.

Mr. Krickleman entered the room. He was carrying the ballot box. He placed the box on a special table that had been set up at the far end of the room. Then he took the cover, with the slot in it, off the box. He emptied the ballots on the table. He started counting the ballots, and writing on a piece of paper. Maggie tried to figure out how he was doing what he was doing. She strained to see if there were a big pile of ballots and a little pile of ballots, but the box was in the way. Mr. Krickleman was talking to himself. Whatever he was doing with the ballots, he was doing twice or three times or even four times. He put his fingers through his hair, he wiped his nose, he loosened his necktie and he kept counting and writing. At last he looked up and announced, "I have counted and recounted the ballots to make certain there was no error. And now, members of the sixth grade, we have a winner! You have a president." Mr. Krickleman tightened the tie he had just loosened. He said, "When I announce the winner's name, will that person please come forward and say a few words to the class."

Maggie felt she couldn't wait another second. She couldn't breathe. She longed for the ordinary, plain moments of her life.

"Your new president," said Mr. Krickleman, "is NOAH MOORE!!!"

"Noah?" said Maggie. "Noah?"

"I don't believe it. I don't believe it!" said Noah.

Most of the sixth grade was cheering wildly.

Maggie looked over to the next table. Thad and Henry appeared to be in deep shock.

"Come, Noah, speech! Speech!" called Mr. Krickleman.

Noah got up. Slowly, as if his legs had been

given a new job that they had no previous experience for, he walked toward Mr. Krickleman.

"Poor Noah," said Ellen to Maggie. "Down deep he's still a scared person. And I think I know what he's going to say to the class. He'll say, 'Thank you. I quit.'"

"No, he won't," said Maggie. "Noah will say, 'Thank you for the great honor you have bestowed upon me. Unfortunately, I am unable to fulfill the functions of the presidency of this class. I therefore resign.'"

Noah was now standing beside Mr. Krickleman, who shook his hand.

Noah turned and faced the class. He said, "Thank you. I accept."

22

A Different Kind of Victory

Another great cheer went up for Noah. Maggie couldn't believe it. She couldn't believe anything. Noah elected as president! Noah saying, "I accept." I *accept*. How could he accept? He was her campaign manager. More than that, he was her friend.

"I can't believe it," Maggie said to Ellen.

"Go up and tell Noah you can't believe it," said Ellen. "See what he says. And if it's any help, tell him I can't believe it either."

Maggie walked up to Noah, who was still standing facing the class. Everyone was looking at Maggie as she walked up to Noah. But Maggie didn't even notice.

"Noah," she whispered when she got beside him, "I don't believe this. Either does Ellen."

Noah whispered back, "Count me in. I don't believe it, either. But Maggie, I want to tell you something immediately. I'm not really accepting.

I'm too frightened *not* to accept right now. I can't get up in front of everybody here and tell them that the object of their enthusiasm does not want to be president."

"You mean you don't *want* to be president?"

"It never crossed my mind. I enjoyed being your manager. I wanted *you* to win."

Mr. Krickleman and the class were staring at Maggie and Noah. Why would they be standing in the middle of the room whispering to each other?

"Louder, louder," shouted Ronald. "We want to hear."

"Be quiet, Ronald," said Maggie. "This is private."

"Private in the middle of the lunchroom?" said Ronald. "Ridiculous. Everybody who wants to hear, raise your hand."

Hands shot up all over the room. Even Ellen raised hers.

Noah whispered to Maggie. "I failed as a manager when I wanted to succeed and I succeeded as a presidential candidate when I wasn't even running. And I messed up your campaign."

"You didn't mess it up," Maggie whispered. "I know why you got elected."

"Tell me," said Noah.

"Louder," shouted Ronald.

Maggie turned toward Mr. Krickleman. "May I speak to the class?" she asked.

"Anything," said Mr. Krickleman, "that would quiet Ronald would be greatly appreciated."

"Class," said Maggie, "I wanted to be president. And Thad Smith, who was a fair and honest opponent, also wanted to be president. But Noah should be president. He knows the most about what the sixth grade needs. And you know it. And that's why you voted for him."

Ronald yelled, "You're hogging the show, Maggie. Let Thad talk, too."

Henry pulled Thad up from his seat and gave him a slight push toward the center of the room.

Then Thad, Maggie and Noah were standing together in the middle of the room.

Thad spoke to the class. "I have three things to say. If you want Noah for president, it's okay with me. That's the first thing. The second thing is that I am still fair and honest. The third thing is that Maggie Marmelstein is sometimes great. The reason I said the third thing is because the second thing is true."

Maggie felt wonderful. She also felt victorious. But not victorious over anyone. How could that be? Maybe there were different kinds of victories, and you couldn't campaign for some of them. They weren't won. They were earned.

Noah whispered to her and Thad. "It is definitely better to lose together than to win separately."

"What do you mean?" asked Maggie.

"I mean I didn't want to be president," said Noah. "That's what I've already told you. But now both of you have told the sixth grade that you support me. Now I can't resign simply. I'll have to resign complicatedly."

"How do you do that?" asked Thad.

"I don't know," said Noah. "It's going to be hard work. It's going to be the most difficult work I've ever done."

Noah shook Maggie's hand and Thad's hand. Then he left the lunchroom before anyone could catch up with him.

The class slowly left after him.

Maggie and Thad walked home together. "Well, Noah is president," said Maggie. "For weeks and weeks and weeks. It will take him all that time to do an absolutely first-rate job of resigning. He'll search for all kinds of information, he'll go to every library in the area, he'll send for booklets from the government, he'll rehearse and he'll rehearse again. He might even consult zodiac signs."

"Then what happens?" asked Thad. "If he finally resigns?"

"A new election, I guess," said Maggie.

"Would you run again?" asked Thad.

"Maybe," said Maggie. "Would you?"

"Maybe," said Thad.

Maggie and Thad reached their apartment house.

"Want some victory cake?" asked Maggie.

"Why not?" said Thad.

Victory Cake

Ingredients

1 cup pumpkin (half of a 1-lb. can)
½ cup brown sugar
6 cut-up or torn-apart dates
1 banana, mashed
1 small grab of raisins
ditto sunflower seeds
1 very big grab of cut-up pecans or walnuts
½ cup whole wheat flour
a few drops of orange juice
ditto sweet red wine
1 slight shake of salt
½ teaspoon baking soda
1 tablespoon baking powder
2 eggs

1 pan: about size 9" x 5" x 3" will do nicely, but a little smaller is okay, too.

For the pan

Some butter or margarine to grease its insides, and then a few shakes of wheat germ to sprinkle over what's greased. Sprinkle carefully so that all the sprinkles aren't in one place. The sides might not easily accept sprinkles, but the bottom will.

Instructions

Mix all the above ingredients (except the pan ingredients) in a mixing bowl. Don't hesitate to give the mixture some hits and pushes. But perfectly smooth it won't be. Expect lumps, bumps and stick-outs.

After it looks like the above description, consider it mixed up. Then put the mixture into the pan, which I hope you have already greased and wheat-germed. Bake in a 350° oven for about three quarters of an hour.

Sometimes the cake tastes better cold than warm. First you can try it warm because it will be warm first. Then you can wait a day or so and try it cold if you want.

The cake will feed three or four people who are crazy about it, or five or six people who are somewhere between crazy about it and liking it quite a bit, or seven-plus people who are somewhere between liking it quite a bit and no-thank-you. Or any combination you can work out.